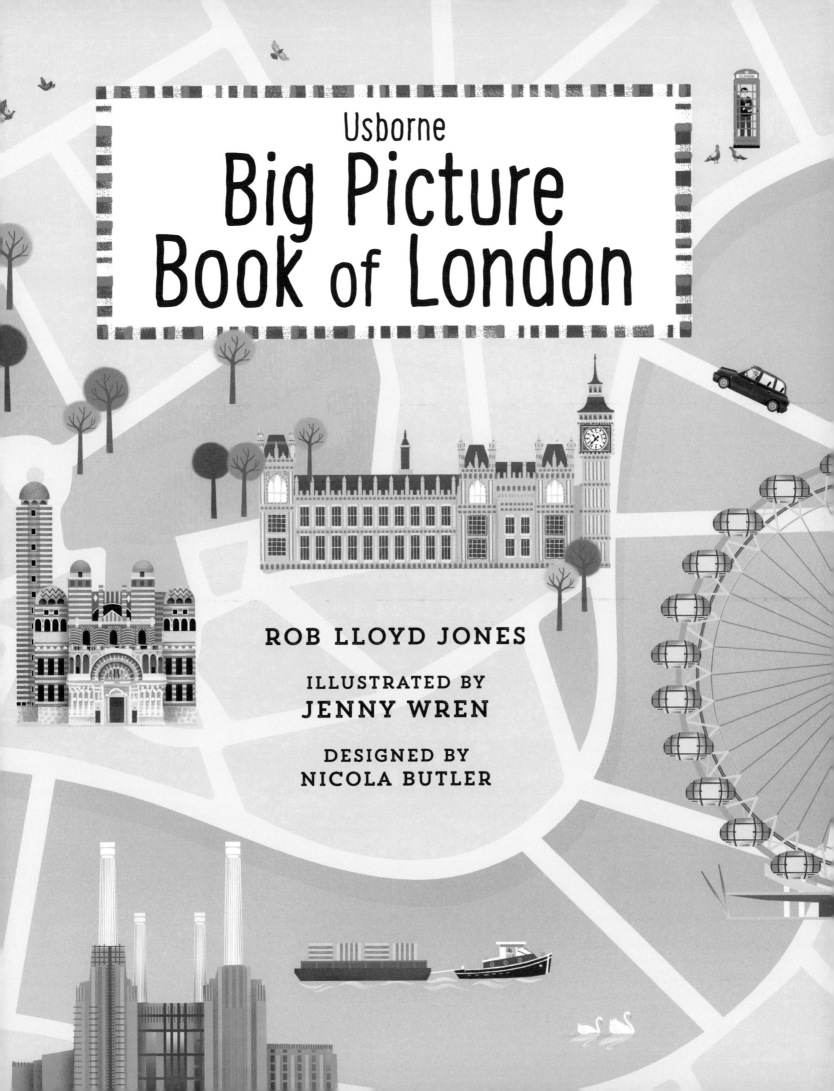

Usborne
Big Picture
Book of London

ROB LLOYD JONES

ILLUSTRATED BY
JENNY WREN

DESIGNED BY
NICOLA BUTLER

CONTENTS

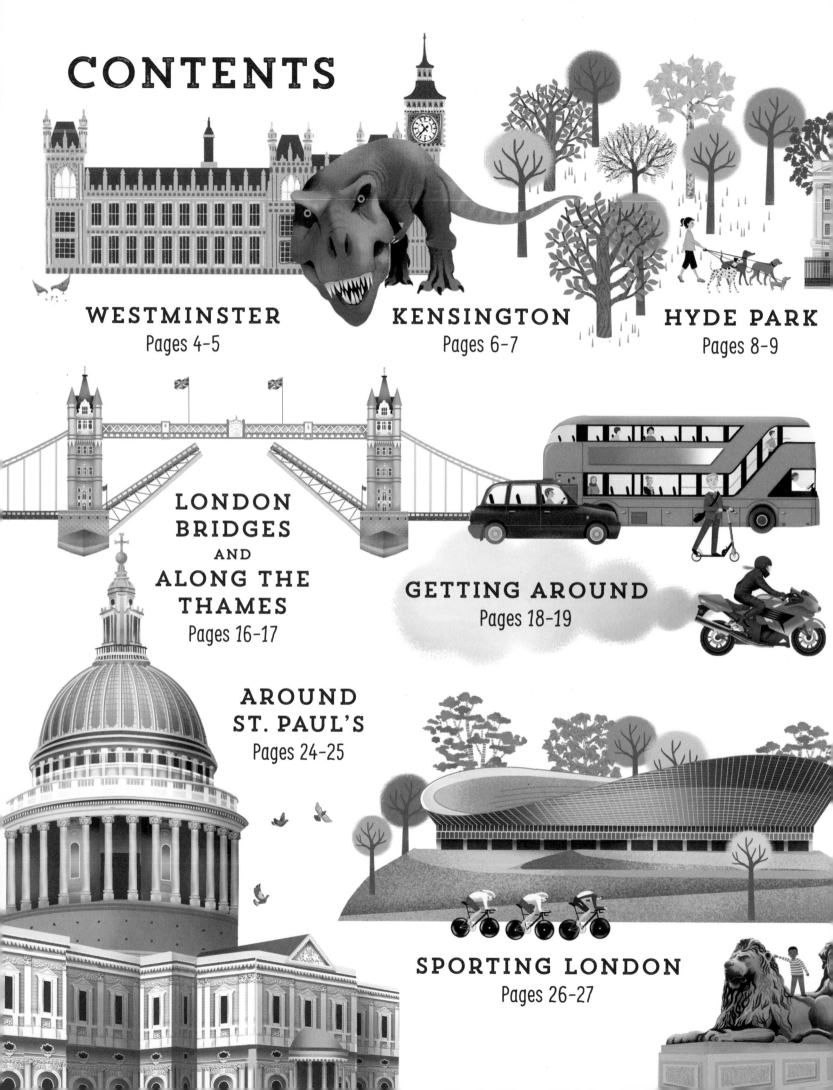

INTERNET LINKS
To find out more about London, its history and famous sights, go to www.usborne.com/quicklinks and type in the keywords 'big picture book of london'.

St. James's Park

WESTMINSTER

This area of London is the home of the British government, where politicians work. There are also two grand churches here. Glittering royal ceremonies take place in Westminster Abbey.

No. 10 Downing Street

The British Prime Minister lives here. No. 10 Downing Street is actually three houses joined together, with over 100 rooms inside.

Westminster Cathedral

This cathedral is the headquarters of the Roman Catholic Church in Britain.

Churchill statue

Sir Winston Churchill was the British Prime Minister during the Second World War.

CHURCHILL

Parliament Square

Westminster Abbey

Kings and queens have been crowned in this church for around 1,000 years. Most of them are buried here, too.

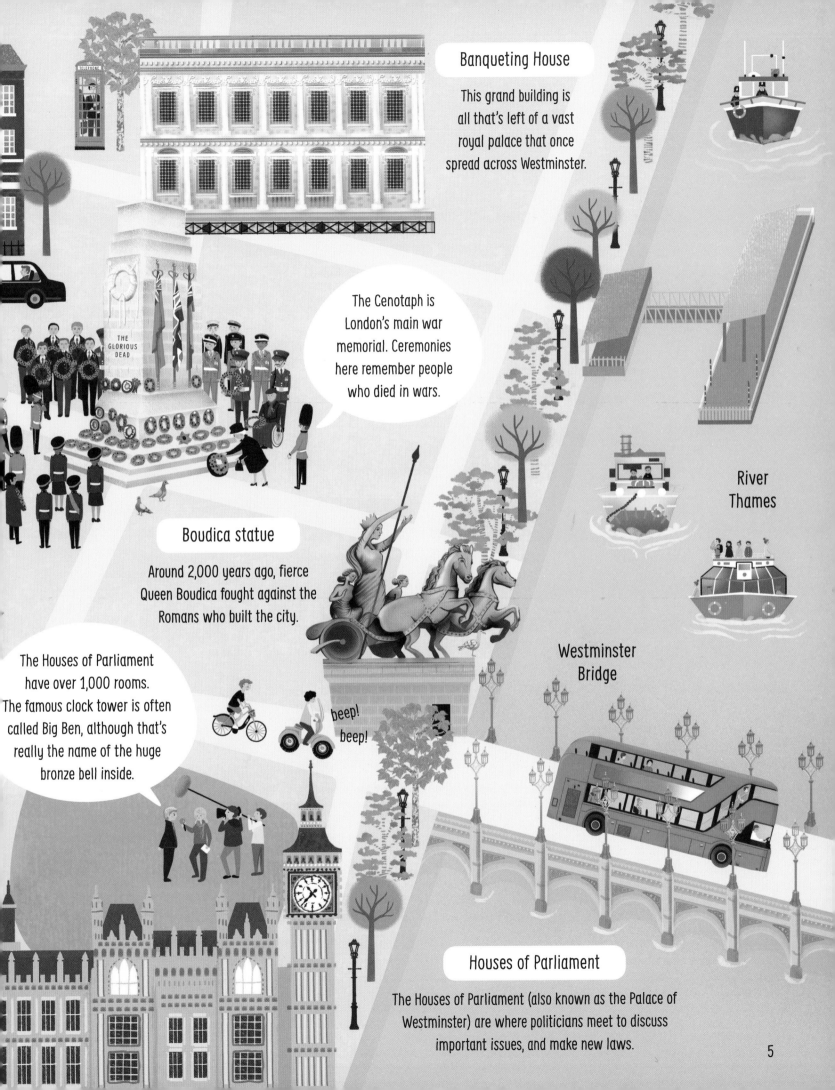

Banqueting House

This grand building is all that's left of a vast royal palace that once spread across Westminster.

THE GLORIOUS DEAD

The Cenotaph is London's main war memorial. Ceremonies here remember people who died in wars.

River Thames

Boudica statue

Around 2,000 years ago, fierce Queen Boudica fought against the Romans who built the city.

Westminster Bridge

The Houses of Parliament have over 1,000 rooms. The famous clock tower is often called Big Ben, although that's really the name of the huge bronze bell inside.

beep! beep!

Houses of Parliament

The Houses of Parliament (also known as the Palace of Westminster) are where politicians meet to discuss important issues, and make new laws.

5

Kensington
Gardens

Albert
Memorial

Royal Geographical Society

Explorers meet here
to plan expeditions to
far-off places.

Science Museum

This museum is packed with
displays about the history
and the future of science.

The Royal Albert Hall

Concerts and shows are held at
this oval-shaped hall.

INSIDE THE NATURAL
HISTORY MUSEUM

The skeleton
of a blue whale

A Tyrannosaurus
rex model

17 million
creepy
crawlies

SCIENCE

Natural History Museum

Here you can see wonders from the
natural world — animals, plants,
rocks and fossils.

Harrods department store

Harrods has 330 'departments' selling all sorts of unusual and luxury goods. The Pet Department once sold a baby elephant.

Most of London's big museums and galleries are free to visit.

KENSINGTON

Museums and galleries sit side-by-side in this part of London. You can see fascinating things from the all around the world, from dinosaur bones to the very latest technology.

INSIDE THE SCIENCE MUSEUM

The first ever steam train

Spacecraft

Science experiments

INSIDE THE V&A

Ancient sculptures...

...and modern sculptures too

Strange models

Historical costumes

Victoria and Albert Museum (V&A)

This museum of art and design displays sculpture, fashion and furniture.

HYDE PARK

London has lots of leafy parks, big and small, where people relax and escape the noise of the busy roads. This is the city's biggest park, Hyde Park.

Pretty fountains

Pirate playground

This area of the park is called Kensington Gardens.

Arrgh!

Peter Pan statue

Peter Pan's magical adventures were partly set in this park.

Kensington Palace

For over 300 years, different members of the Royal Family have lived at this palace.

Round Pond

Serpentine Gallery

The Albert Memorial

This memorial is dedicated to Queen Victoria's husband, Prince Albert.

BUCKINGHAM PALACE

This palace is the official home of British kings and queens. Every morning, new soldiers come on duty here, in a ceremony called the Changing the Guard.

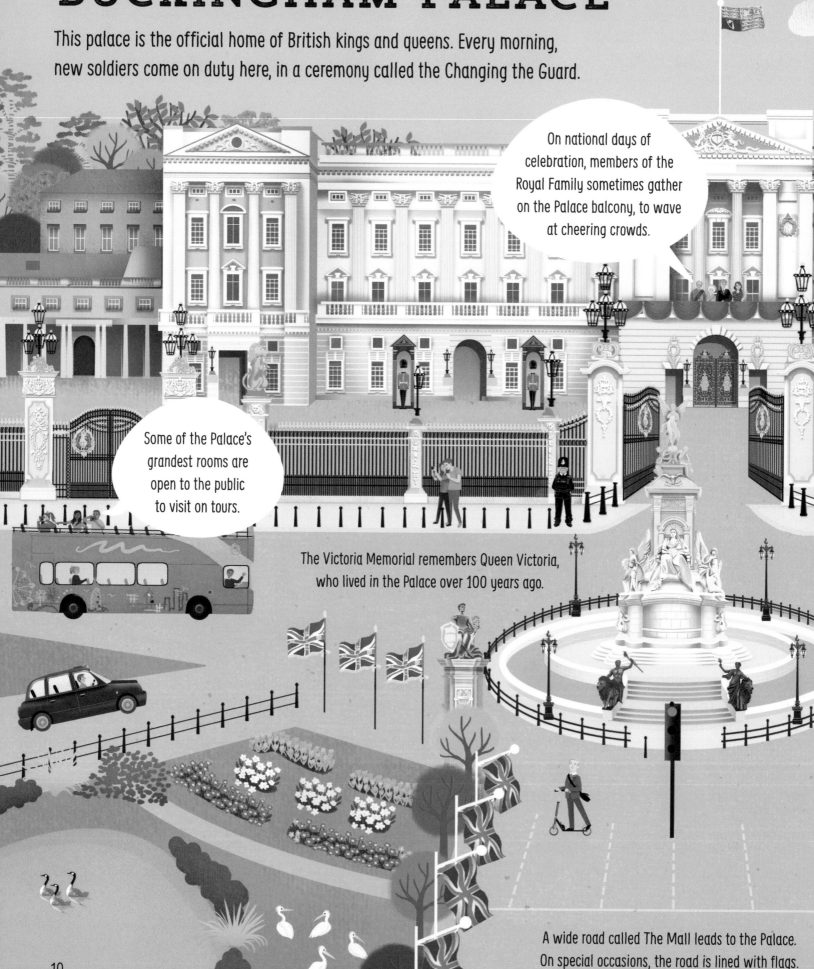

On national days of celebration, members of the Royal Family sometimes gather on the Palace balcony, to wave at cheering crowds.

Some of the Palace's grandest rooms are open to the public to visit on tours.

The Victoria Memorial remembers Queen Victoria, who lived in the Palace over 100 years ago.

A wide road called The Mall leads to the Palace. On special occasions, the road is lined with flags.

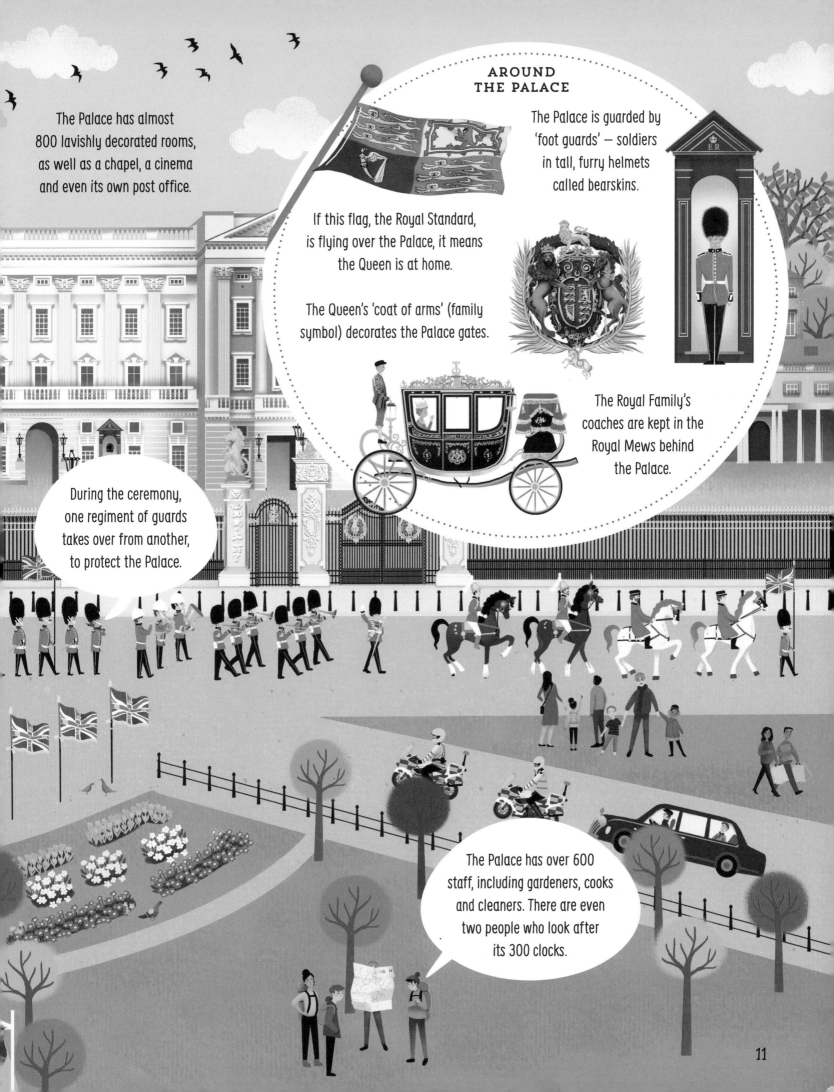

The Palace has almost 800 lavishly decorated rooms, as well as a chapel, a cinema and even its own post office.

AROUND THE PALACE

If this flag, the Royal Standard, is flying over the Palace, it means the Queen is at home.

The Queen's 'coat of arms' (family symbol) decorates the Palace gates.

The Palace is guarded by 'foot guards' – soldiers in tall, furry helmets called bearskins.

The Royal Family's coaches are kept in the Royal Mews behind the Palace.

During the ceremony, one regiment of guards takes over from another, to protect the Palace.

The Palace has over 600 staff, including gardeners, cooks and cleaners. There are even two people who look after its 300 clocks.

ROYAL LONDON

London has been home to British kings and queens for around 1,000 years. Today there are several lavish palaces around the city.

Buckingham Palace

Marble Arch

This marble gateway was moved from Buckingham Palace to the corner of Hyde Park, around 150 years ago.

This red-brick gatehouse is one of the oldest parts of St. James's Palace.

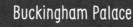

St. James's Palace

St. James's Palace was home to King Henry VIII and then his daughter, Queen Elizabeth I, around 500 years ago.

Kensington Palace

Diana, Princess of Wales, once lived in this palace, which is at the end of Kensington Gardens.

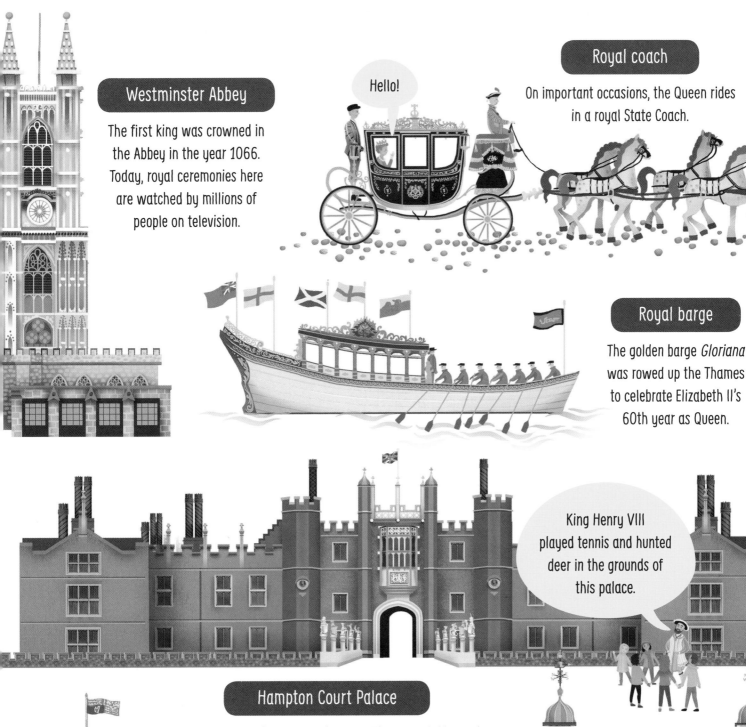

Westminster Abbey

The first king was crowned in the Abbey in the year 1066. Today, royal ceremonies here are watched by millions of people on television.

Hello!

Royal coach

On important occasions, the Queen rides in a royal State Coach.

Royal barge

The golden barge *Gloriana* was rowed up the Thames to celebrate Elizabeth II's 60th year as Queen.

King Henry VIII played tennis and hunted deer in the grounds of this palace.

Hampton Court Palace

Hampton Court, on the bank of the River Thames outside London, was another of King Henry VIII's homes.

Windsor Castle

The Queen sometimes spends weekends at this grand castle outside London.

The Tower of London

GOING UP...

Lots of interesting buildings poke up around London's skyline.
Here are some of the tallest...

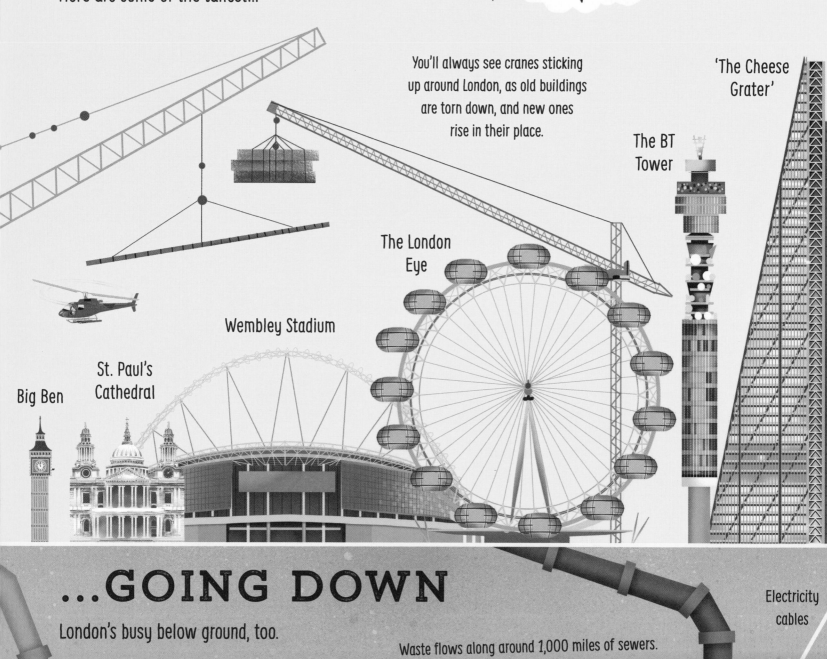

You'll always see cranes sticking up around London, as old buildings are torn down, and new ones rise in their place.

'The Cheese Grater'

The BT Tower

The London Eye

Wembley Stadium

St. Paul's Cathedral

Big Ben

...GOING DOWN

London's busy below ground, too.

Waste flows along around 1,000 miles of sewers.

Electricity cables

Londoners get around by underground train. The city has almost 300 underground stations.

14

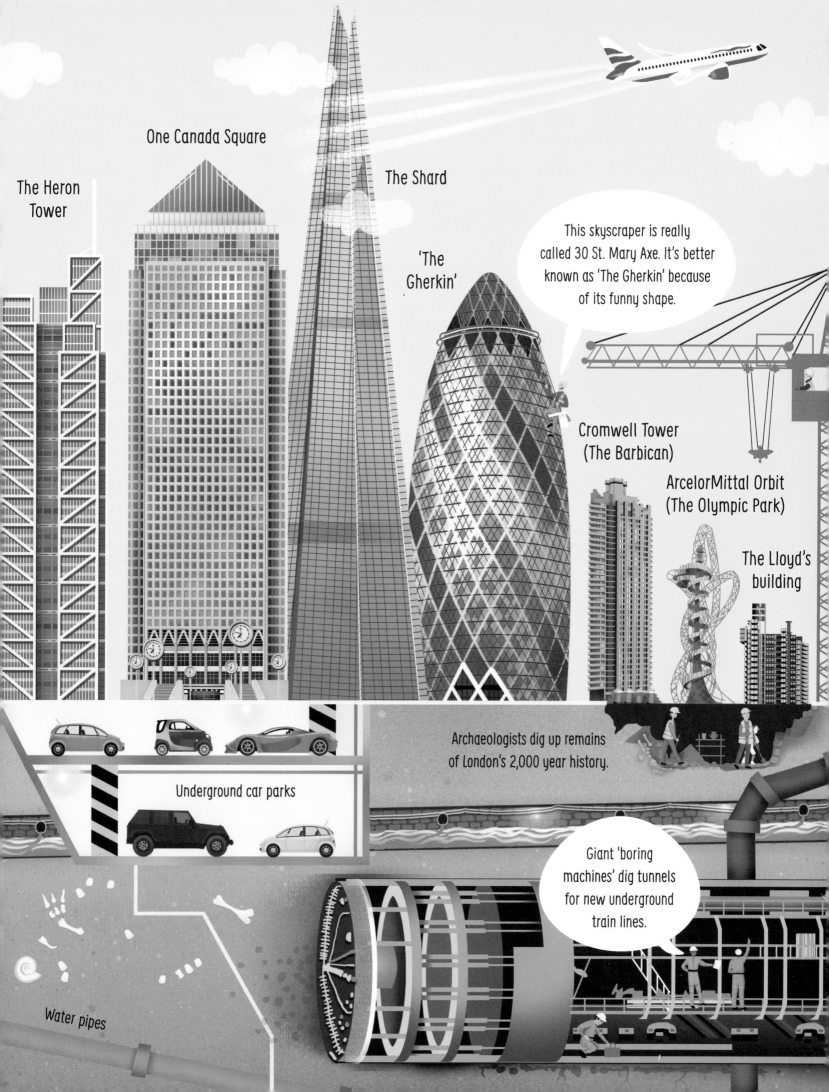

Somerset House

Dukes and queens once lived in this grand mansion. Today it's used for exhibitions and outdoor concerts.

St. Paul's Cathedral

Tate Modern

This old power station is one of London's largest and most popular art galleries.

Oxo Tower

The Golden Hind

This is a copy of a ship that set sail from London around 400 years ago, on an epic journey around the world. Its captain was the explorer Sir Francis Drake.

Shakespeare's Globe

This is a copy of a playhouse called the Globe, where many of William Shakespeare's plays were first performed over 400 years ago.

William Shakespeare was one of the owners of the original Globe playhouse.

The London Eye

This huge observation wheel carries people in glass capsules, for amazing views across the city.

Southwark Cathedral

ALONG THE THAMES

The River Thames winds through London, with famous landmarks lining its banks. Tourists take boats up and down the river, to see all the sights.

Nelson's Column

Cleopatra's Needle

Named after an Ancient Egyptian queen, this obelisk was a gift from Egypt to Britain. It's over 3,500 years old.

The Houses of Parliament

Tate Britain

This gallery displays British paintings, sculptures and photographs.

The London Eye was only meant to be up for five years, but it was so popular it wasn't taken down.

Battersea Power Station

The white chimneys of this old power station are a famous London landmark.

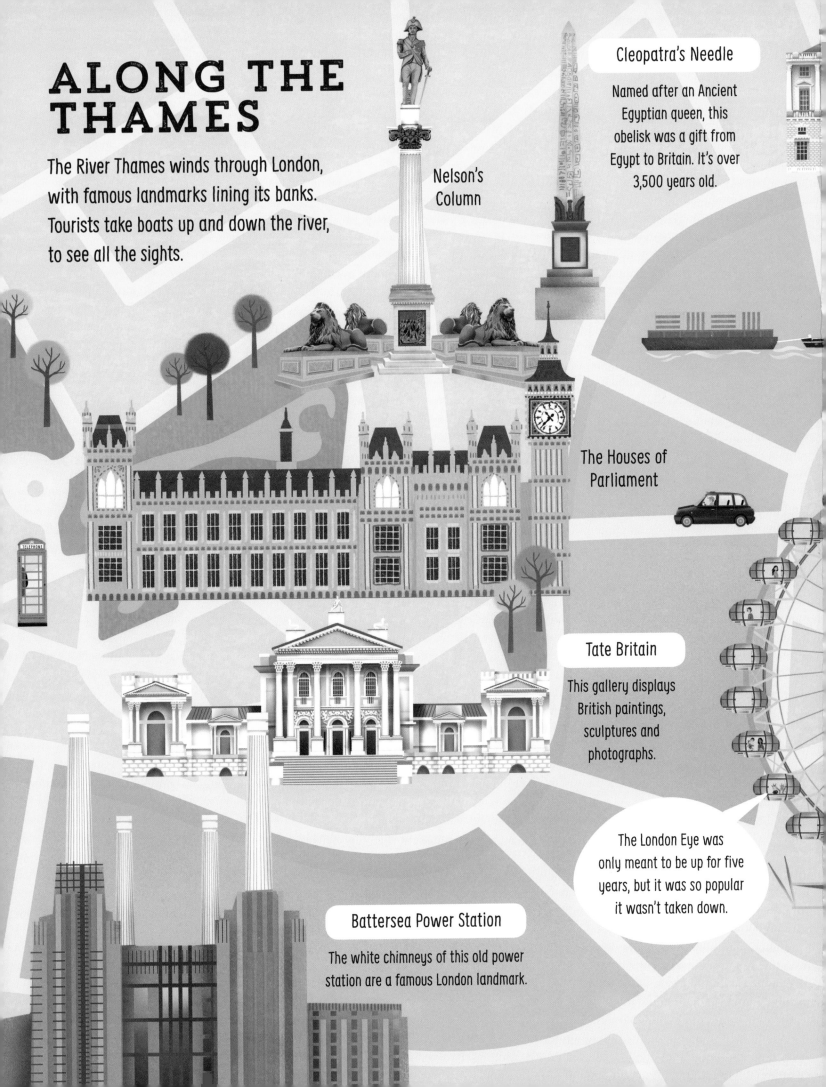

LONDON BRIDGES

These are some of the the bridges that cross the River Thames in Central London...

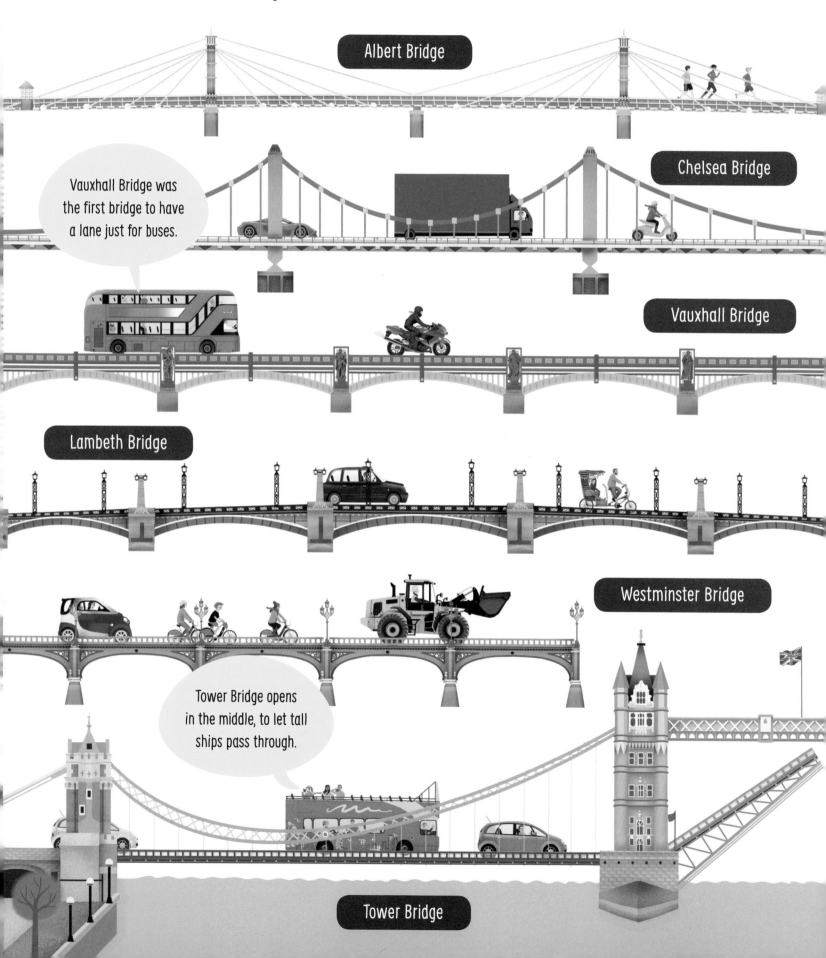

GETTING AROUND

Beep beep! People get around London in all sorts of different ways — on roads, rivers, train tracks, and even up in the air.

Helicopter

Some of London's buildings have platforms on the roof, for helicopters to take off and land.

Whiirrrllllll

Double decker bus

Red 'double decker' buses are a famous London sight.

Bicycle

Police horse

Tourists snap photos from buses with open top decks.

Pedicab

riiing!

Motorbike

Sightseeing bus

London Underground

Underground trains speed through tunnels beneath London.

Aldgate   5mins

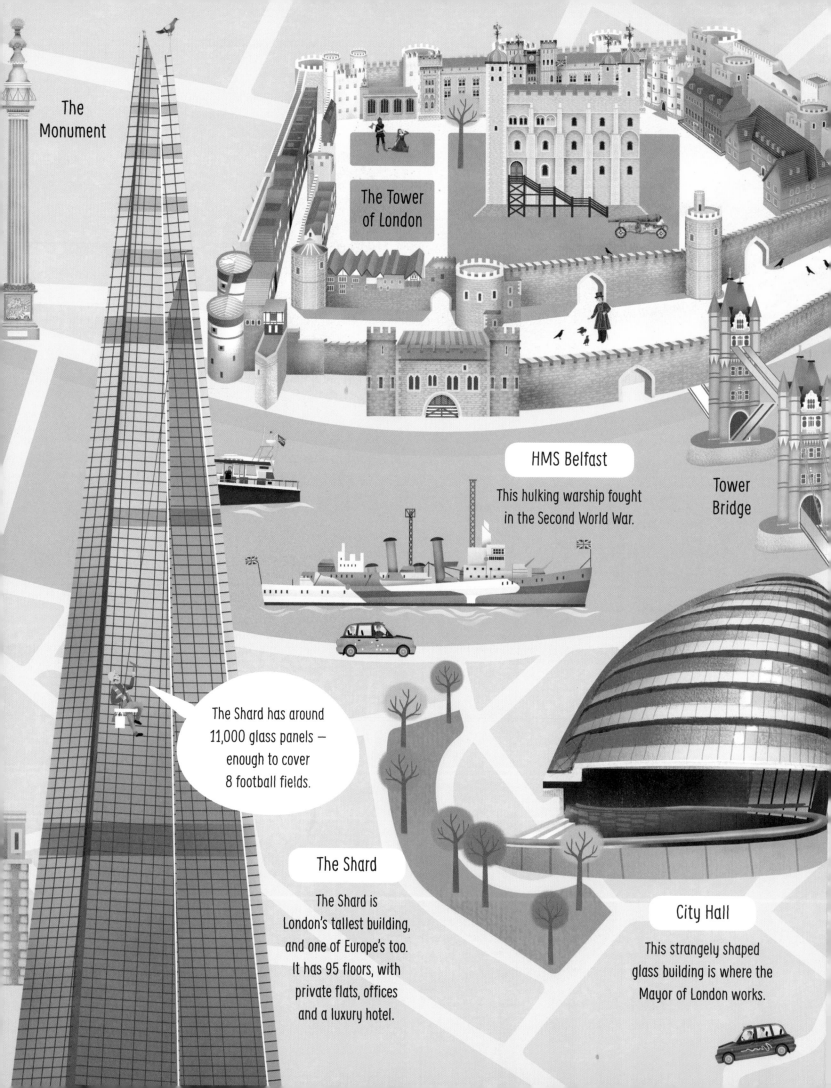

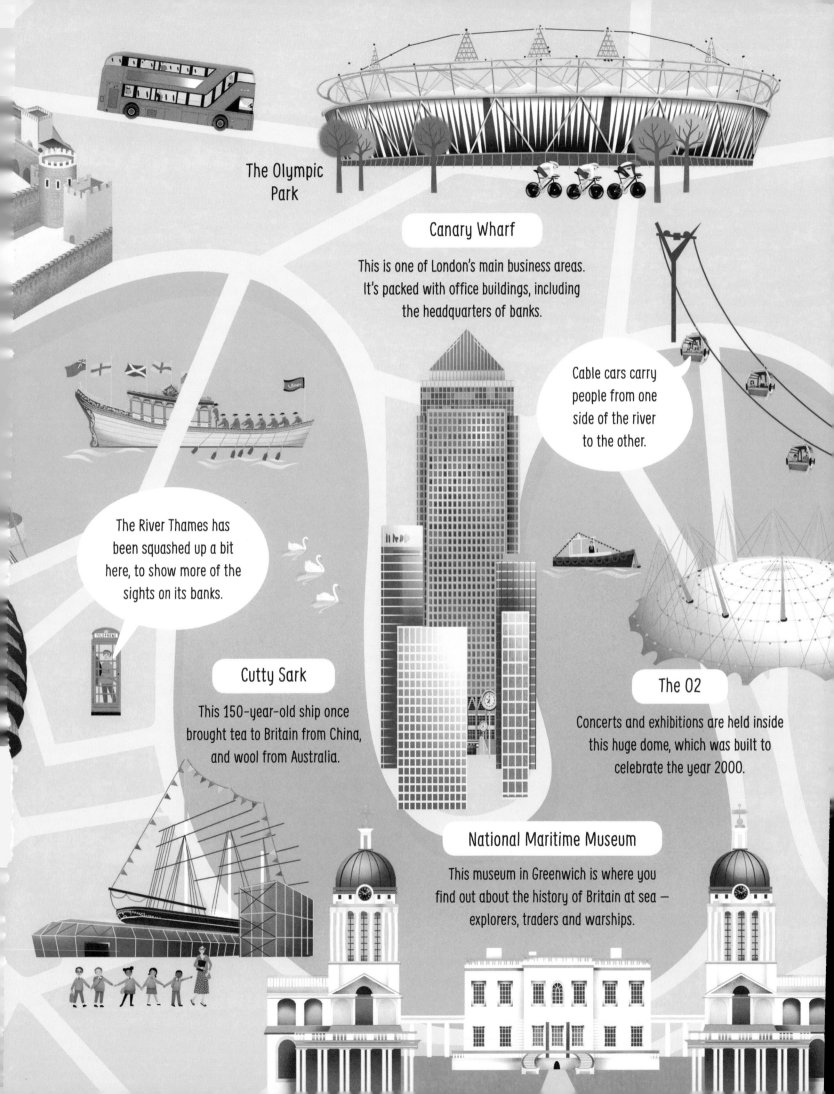

The Olympic Park

Canary Wharf

This is one of London's main business areas. It's packed with office buildings, including the headquarters of banks.

Cable cars carry people from one side of the river to the other.

The River Thames has been squashed up a bit here, to show more of the sights on its banks.

Cutty Sark

This 150-year-old ship once brought tea to Britain from China, and wool from Australia.

The O2

Concerts and exhibitions are held inside this huge dome, which was built to celebrate the year 2000.

National Maritime Museum

This museum in Greenwich is where you find out about the history of Britain at sea — explorers, traders and warships.

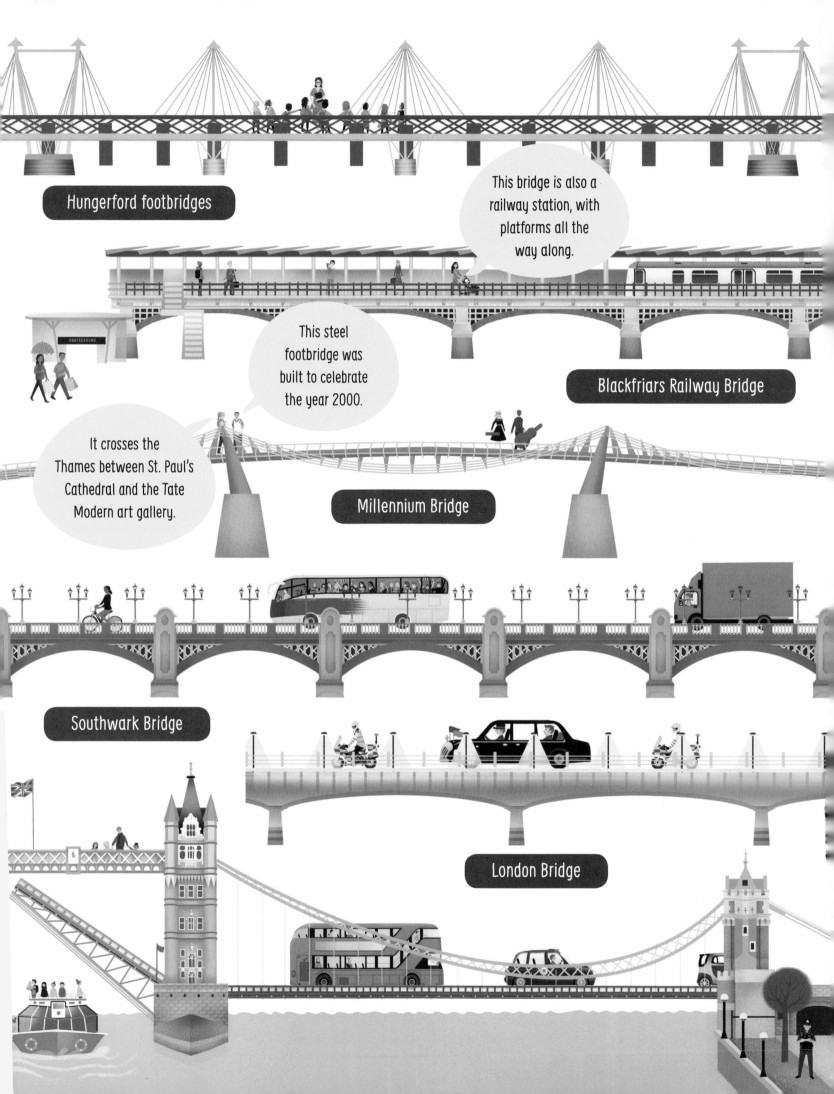

Cable car

A cable car system carries passengers up and over the River Thames in East London.

Great view!

Black cabs whisk people around London's busy streets.

Black cab

beep! beep!

Scooter

Digger

Thames Clipper

These speedy boats carry people to and from work, or on sightseeing trips along the Thames.

Police river boat

Docklands Light Railway trains have no drivers, so you can sit right at the front.

'Duck' boats drive along the roads and then splash into the River Thames.

Vrooommm...

Duck boat

Docklands Light Railway

Chinatown

Chinatown is the heart of London's Chinese community. Its streets are decorated with painted gates.

Eros

A bronze statue, known as Eros, fires an arrow from the top of a fountain in Piccadilly Circus.

Hamleys

Hamleys is the oldest toy shop in the world. It has over 50,000 toys for sale.

Leicester Square

The National Gallery

Over 2,300 paintings, by some of the most famous artists ever, are on display in this free gallery.

Piccadilly Circus

Piccadilly Circus is a busy, bustling junction in the middle of the West End.

Temporary modern sculptures are displayed on this stone plinth.

Trafalgar Square

This famous square was built to celebrate a victory in a sea battle over 200 years ago.

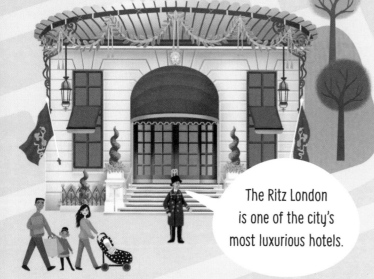

The Ritz London is one of the city's most luxurious hotels.

TRAFALGAR SQUARE

Trafalgar Square is at the heart of London's 'West End' — a buzzy area of shops, restaurants and places to see shows.

St. James's Park

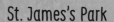

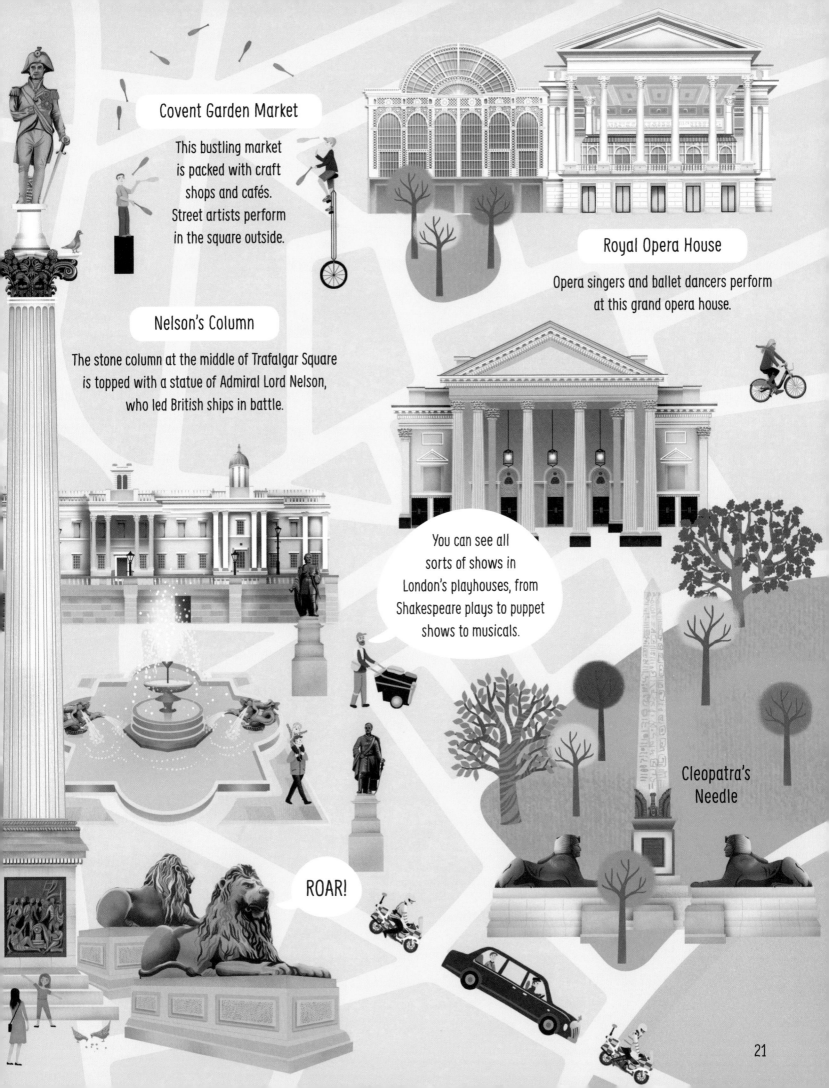

Covent Garden Market

This bustling market is packed with craft shops and cafés. Street artists perform in the square outside.

Royal Opera House

Opera singers and ballet dancers perform at this grand opera house.

Nelson's Column

The stone column at the middle of Trafalgar Square is topped with a statue of Admiral Lord Nelson, who led British ships in battle.

You can see all sorts of shows in London's playhouses, from Shakespeare plays to puppet shows to musicals.

Cleopatra's Needle

ROAR!

Some people say the Tower is haunted...

The White Tower is the oldest part of the fortress. It was once painted bright white.

INSIDE THE TOWER

You can see the priceless Crown Jewels of kings and queens, in the Tower's Jewel House.

Battle suits and weapons are on show. This steel suit belonged to King Henry VIII.

The Tower's guards are known as Beefeaters (possibly because they were once paid with beef).

Today they give tours of the Tower, dressed in red or blue uniforms.

Seven ravens live at the Tower. Legend says if they ever fly away, the Tower will collapse...

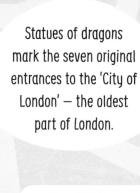

Statues of dragons mark the seven original entrances to the 'City of London' – the oldest part of London.

AROUND ST. PAUL'S

St. Paul's Cathedral is in the City of London, the area once inside the ancient Roman city walls. It's surrounded by fascinating sights.

The Old Bailey

This is Britain's main court for criminal trials. The golden statue at the top is called Lady Justice.

St. Paul's Cathedral

The soaring dome of St. Paul's is one of the biggest in the world.

St. Bride's Church

The stepped steeple of this church may have inspired the tiered design of wedding cakes.

This cathedral was designed by Sir Christopher Wren, who built 51 other churches in London, too.

This is a statue of Queen Anne, who ruled Britain over 300 years ago.

INSIDE ST. PAUL'S CATHEDRAL

Golden mosaics on the ceilings are made up of around 30 million tiny pieces of glass.

HORATIO.VISC.N

MUSEUM OF LONDON

London Wall

You can still see parts of a 2,000-year-old wall that the Romans built around London.

Museum of London

This is the place to find out all about London's glorious and grisly past.

The golden cross at the top of the dome weighs the same as seven cars.

The Guildhall

This is one of the city's oldest buildings. People used to meet here to set prices for buying and selling things.

This is the second cathedral built here called St. Paul's. The first burned down in 1666, during the Great Fire of London.

Bank of England

The Bank of England looks after the British government's money. It has 300,000 gold bars in its vaults.

The Monument

This stone column was built as a memorial to the Great Fire of London, which destroyed most of London around 350 years ago.

A monument to Sir Christopher Wren

e tomb of Admiral ord Nelson is in e crypt (cellar) beneath the cathedral.

A statue of the military leader the Duke of Wellington

SPORTING LONDON

London has lots of famous venues for sports and games...

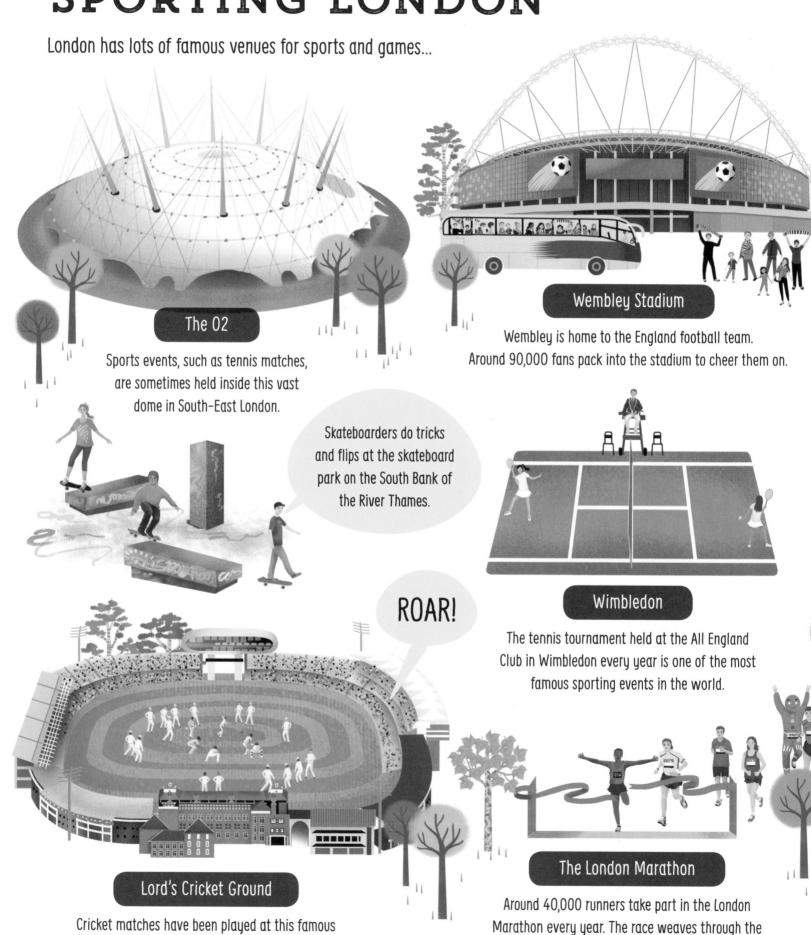

The O2

Sports events, such as tennis matches, are sometimes held inside this vast dome in South-East London.

Wembley Stadium

Wembley is home to the England football team. Around 90,000 fans pack into the stadium to cheer them on.

Skateboarders do tricks and flips at the skateboard park on the South Bank of the River Thames.

ROAR!

Wimbledon

The tennis tournament held at the All England Club in Wimbledon every year is one of the most famous sporting events in the world.

Lord's Cricket Ground

Cricket matches have been played at this famous ground for over 200 years.

The London Marathon

Around 40,000 runners take part in the London Marathon every year. The race weaves through the city, to the finish line outside Buckingham Palace.

The Olympic Park

In 2012, the Olympic and Paralympic Games were held in London. An Olympic Park was built with a stadium for athletics events, as well as venues for hockey, basketball, and all sorts of other sports.

Speedy cycling races take place at the Park's Velodrome.

Swimming and diving competitions are held at the Park's sleek-looking Aquatics Centre.

A twisting metal observation tower gives sports fans views across the Olympic Park.

Every year, rowing teams from Oxford and Cambridge University race each other along the River Thames.

Twickenham

Twickenham Stadium is the home ground of the England rugby team.

OTHER THINGS TO SEE

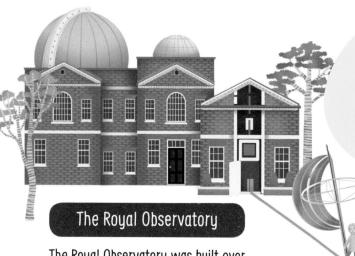

The 'Prime Meridian' line runs through the Observatory, dividing the world into east and west.

The Royal Observatory

The Royal Observatory was built over 300 years ago, for astronomers to study the stars. Today it's a museum.

Imperial War Museum

You can see guns, tanks and planes at this museum, and find out what life was like in London in wartime.

The British Museum

The British Museum is the oldest national public museum in the world, and one of the biggest.

Here you can walk through an underwater tunnel, with all sorts of sea life around you.

The London Aquarium

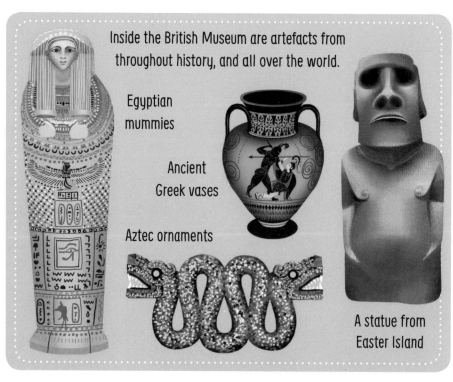

Inside the British Museum are artefacts from throughout history, and all over the world.

Egyptian mummies

Ancient Greek vases

Aztec ornaments

A statue from Easter Island

London Zoo

London Zoo is home to over 7,000 animals, from tiny insects to mighty gorillas.

MONKEY WALK

REPTILE HOUSE

AQUARIUM

Regent's Canal flows through the north of London.

Primrose Hill

Regent's Canal

29

THE HISTORY OF LONDON

In the last 2,000 years London has survived invasions, attacks, plagues and fires, to become one of the the biggest cities in the world.

TUDOR TIMES
Hampton Court Palace and St. James's Palace were built.

MIDDLE AGES
London was a busy, bustling city. London Bridge was lined with houses. Each year, a new mayor was chosen at the Guildhall.

ROMANS
The Romans invaded Britain. They built a town beside the River Thames, called *Londinium*, with a wall all the way around.

INVASION!
Normans, from France, invaded Britain. Later, the Tower of London was built as a royal palace.

SAXONS AND VIKINGS
The Saxons, who came from Germany, battled for control of London with Danish Vikings.

the 1500s

by 1400

1066

400-1000

2,000 years ago

ELIZABETH'S LONDON
During the reign of Queen Elizabeth I, London was a mix of lavish palaces, and rowdy inns and playhouses.

WESTMINSTER ABBEY...
...was built during this period, by Saxon King Edward the Confessor.

This is the *Globe* playhouse.

PLAGUE AND FIRE

London was ravaged by a disease called the Great Plague. Then, the Great Fire of London burned down most of the city.

LONDON IS REBUILT

St. Paul's Cathedral was built, and the British Museum opened.

VICTORIAN LONDON

Queen Victoria moved into Buckingham Palace. The Houses of Parliament were built, as well as museums such as the V&A.

TODAY

Around 8 million people live in London. Striking new office buildings such as 30 St. Mary Axe and the Shard stand beside famous buildings from the city's past.

MILLENNIUM

The London Eye was built, as well as the Millennium Bridge and the O2 arena.

THE BLITZ

During the Second World War, London was bombed by enemy planes in what was known as 'the Blitz'.

1665-1666

the 1700s

the 1800s

the 1940s

2000

today

THE MONUMENT

This column was built near London Bridge, to remember the Great Fire.

St. Paul's Cathedral was completed to Sir Christopher Wren's designs in 1711.

IN 2012...

...the Olympic Games were held in London. New sports arenas were built for the events, including the Olympic Stadium.

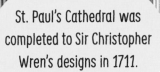